MANAGING ONLINE ACCOUNTS

Creating, managing, and tracking Internet online accounts

Contents

Introduction

Before the Internet was in widespread use (sometime before 1996), the problem of maintaining a multitude of account names and passwords didn't exist. However, some people kept a log of their acquaintances' or friends' home addresses and phone numbers using an address book.

After the Internet became widespread and commercialized, people began to create many accounts—first with their Internet Service Provider's (ISP's) account, then various free email accounts from providers like Yahoo, Microsoft, and Google. As the use of the web became more accessible to everyone, businesses such as banks and online stores began to make their services available through the web as well.

In 2004, a social networking company called Facebook entered the scene. Soon after Google came up with google plus, and other companies came up with other social networking-type service like MySpace, Twitter, Instagram, Pinterest, and many others.

Today, everything we do on the web requires one form of an account or another. Even the games people play on the Internet require some form of login. So it isn't too farfetched to say that anyone who is connected to the Web has at least 20 accounts!

That said, unless you make all your accounts exactly the same or you have a super photographic memory, you'll need someplace to write down or record all your account information.

This book answers the question of where to save your account and other relevant information, how to create hard to guess passwords that you can easily remember, and how to secure that information even if someone else finds it.

Lastly, this book provides you with enough space to store your important information.

Saving Account Information

Since we have a need to record our accounts and various related information, the question of where we should save such information is the first we need to answer.

There are two general options here: write the information on paper or enter them into an electronic form via some app or application.

Save Accounts in Electronic Form

Saving account and related information in electronic form is great because it is extremely easy to replicate the information and store them in various location. This same advantage can be a hindrance if you aren't able to synchronize copies of the data. Not only that, in order to read your data, you need a powered electronic device. Without it, you cannot access and read your data. In addition, if you store your data on a physical hard disk drive or flash drive, it is just a matter of time before that device fails. When it does, there isn't a guarantee you can recover your data. If you store your data on some online storage service or free storage such as OneDrive or GDrive, then there is some danger of your data being compromised. After all, whether we like it or not, hacking is part of online life.

Save Accounts on Paper

A more natural way of storing your information is to write them on paper. Not just on any paper, but on a paged or tabbed notebook like the one you are holding now.

The main drawback is that if you lose the notebook, you'll have to depend on your memory to recover your lost data. On top of that, if someone else finds it, they will have all your account secrets!

There is a way to prevent a disaster like that. You need to be vigilant about handling your precious account data. First of all, you need a safe place to hide and store it. Next, you need to come up with a scheme to make the information in your log unusable to others unless they know your scheme.

Hard to Guess Passwords

Did you know that with today's computing power hackers can actually "brute force guess" your password? If you use common words and schemes, hackers can do an exhaustive guess of your password through a massive dictionary of common passwords.

To create stronger passwords, use these ideas:

1. Mix into your passwords capital and lower case characters

2. Also use numbers, punctuation marks, and spaces

3. Include the first letter of every word in a passphrase. A passphrase is two or more words that can easily be remembered. For example, for the passphrase "To be or not to be", use **Tbontb** as part of your password.

4. Make your password be at least 8 characters long

Remembering too many accounts and passwords is really a challenge for everyone. The easiest solution for all is to make your accounts all the same, but the problem is that if someone guesses your account information, all of your accounts will be compromised. Not a good scenario.

One way to get around this problem is to use part of the web site's name in a **base password** that you can easily remember. Simply add one or more characters from the web site's name in your base password and place it at the beginning, in the middle, or at the end.

For example, let say you like using Tbontb!1979 as your base password and you would like to use it as your password for your Google.com account. You can simply add "Go" at the beginning of your password like this "**GoTbontb!1979**". Supposing you also have a Yahoo.com account. You can make your password there be "**YaTbontb!1979**". This way you have a way to remember your passwords simply by knowing which site you're visiting and logging into. You can just keep doing this for other sites.

Provided you have a good base password and you can remember it, you can see how easier it is now to remember multiple accounts and passwords. There really is no limit on how many sites where you can apply this technique.

Securing Your Accounts

A safe is an example of what one would use to secure valuables. It is typically placed somewhere in the house where a burglar will not expect to find it. If they do find it, they need to know the combination in order to access the valuables inside.

Securing your account information is like putting your valuables in a safe.

First you need a notepad that doesn't have any writing on its cover that alerts the bad guy that you have accounts and passwords in it.

Next, you need to find a place where you can place this notebook—typically in a physically safe place or in a place where it is mixed in with similar but not valuable items (i.e. hide it in plain sight).

Last but not least, you need to come up with your own scheme to basically make your account information worthless even if someone finds it.

A Notepad

For this part, you are good to go. You can use this book to log your account and various relevant information.

A Hiding Place

I would say that you should hide your notepad in plain sight. If you try to put it in someplace that make it look important, then when someone finds it, that is exactly what they will think—that the contents of the notepad is very valuable.

That said, put it in places where people will expect to find such things. Since you are using this book as the notepad for your account information, then you should put it in your bookshelf, mixed in with other books. This book is a book after all with its book title and all.

A Scheme

In order to make your account information worthless, you need to mix in or omit one or more characters in your account and/or password. Where you add or omit can be up to you. It could be at the beginning, in the middle, at the end, or a mix. Just make sure you remember.

Here are three examples:

What's written	Actual account /password	Scheme used
5Blue!gems	5Bluegems	Insert "!" after 4th character
JFdec1979!	JEFdec1979!	Passwords are prefixed with JEF; omit 2nd character "E"
redDragon$	red**aho**Dragon$	Password is for yahoo.com account; using 3 characters (2nd to 4th) from domain name and placing it starting at 4th character

You can come up with your own scheme; just make sure you are consistent. This way, there is no danger in forgetting your base information as well as the scheme you are using.

Warning

Do not log your security questions on this book. Those password reset/recovery question need not be recorded since you and only you know the answer to them.

Common Accounts

Google.com

Web site: http://www.google.com

A Google account is free. With a Google account you get access to Google's set of web applications to include Google Apps, YouTube, Blogger, Google drive, and Google +.

Account #1

Username	
Password	

Account #2

Username	
Password	

Account #3

Username	
Password	

Account #4

Username	
Password	

Facebook.com

Web site: http://www.facebook.com

Facebook is a social networking site. Setting up an account is free. It is a very easy way to stay in touch with your friends and family. It is also a place where you can follow people, companies, and other organizations that interests you.

Account #1

Username	
Password	

Account #2

Username	
Password	

Account #3

Username	
Password	

Account #4

Username	
Password	

Yahoo.com

Web site: http://www.yahoo.com

An account at Yahoo is free. With it you get email and access to various web applications, similar to Google. Your Yahoo account also gives you access to Flickr—a free 1TB photo storage and sharing site.

Account #1

Username	
Password	

Account #2

Username	
Password	

Account #3

Username	
Password	

Account #4

Username	
Password	

Live.com

Web site: http://www.live.com

Live is like a Google or Yahoo account. It is free
and it provides email and various other web or
online applications. It also provides free online
storage called OneDrive.

Account #1

Username	
Password	

Account #2

Username	
Password	

Account #3

Username	
Password	

Account #4

Username	
Password	

Amazon.com

Web site: http://www.amazon.com

Creating an Amazon account is also free. It is well known as an online shopping site. However, it is also well known to Amazon affiliates as one of the best place to earn online income. For $99/yr you can become a PRIME member with many online benefits (see http://goo.gl/GBONWv).

Account #1

Username	
Password	

Account #2

Username	
Password	

Account #3

Username	
Password	

Account #4

Username	
Password	

Ebay.com

Web site: http://www.ebay.com

Setting up an account on eBay is free. It is an online auction. You can set yourself up as a buyer or seller.

Account #1

Username	
Password	

Account #2

Username	
Password	

Account #3

Username	
Password	

Account #4

Username	
Password	

Twitter.com

Web site: http://www.twitter.com

Twitter is a social networking service as well.
Most people use Twitter to keep abreast of the
latest happenings with people or organizations
they like. Postings on Twitter is limited to 140
characters. So posts tend to be very brief.

Account #1

Username	
Password	

Account #2

Username	
Password	

Account #3

Username	
Password	

Account #4

Username	
Password	

Wordpress.com

Web site: http://www.wordpress.com

WordPress is the number one framework for creating blogs. You can create an account there and establish a blog for free.

Account #1

Username	
Password	

Account #2

Username	
Password	

Account #3

Username	
Password	

Account #4

Username	
Password	

Linkedin.com

Web site: http://www.linkedin.com

LinkedIn is like Facebook, but for professionals. It is used by everyone to find, establish, or maintain professional connections with people in the same field or any field of interest for that matter.

Account #1

Username	
Password	

Account #2

Username	
Password	

Account #3

Username	
Password	

Account #4

Username	
Password	

Craigslist.org

Web site: http://www.craigslist.org

If you want to put an ad online, Craigslist.org is the site to do it on. It is free and very effective. Instead of having a garage sale, do it on Craigslist.

Account #1

Username	
Password	

Account #2

Username	
Password	

Account #3

Username	
Password	

Account #4

Username	
Password	

Tumblr.com

Web site: http://www.tumblr.com

Tumblr is a social blogging service. If you like to blog or follow other bloggers, this is the place to be.

Account #1

Username	
Password	

Account #2

Username	
Password	

Account #3

Username	
Password	

Account #4

Username	
Password	

Alphabetized Section

What follow after this section are alphabetized sections intended for you to fill in with your online accounts. It starts with A and ends in Z.

Supposing you have an account with Bank of America. You would fill in the account fields as follows:

NAME: *Bank of America*	
Web site	*www.bankofamerica.com*
Username	*JohnJones*
Password	Tgif!15tubig
Notes	

Note that the scheme I use here is as follows:

Actual username is "jjones" and actual password is Tgif<u>ank</u>15tubig where "!" is replaced by the 2nd to 4th characters of "<u>ban</u>kofamerica". So even if someone finds this notepad, they'll have the wrong information.

A Apple

NAME:	
Web site	
Username	
Password	
Notes	

NAME:	
Web site	
Username	
Password	
Notes	

NAME:	
Web site	
Username	
Password	
Notes	

NAME:

Web site	
Username	
Password	
Notes	

NAME:

Web site	
Username	
Password	
Notes	

NAME:

Web site	
Username	
Password	
Notes	

NAME:

Web site	
Username	
Password	
Notes	

NAME:

Web site	
Username	
Password	
Notes	

NAME:

Web site	
Username	
Password	
Notes	

NAME:

Web site	
Username	
Password	
Notes	

NAME:

Web site	
Username	
Password	
Notes	

NAME:

Web site	
Username	
Password	
Notes	

NAME:

Web site	
Username	
Password	
Notes	

NAME:

Web site	
Username	
Password	
Notes	

NAME:

Web site	
Username	
Password	
Notes	

NAME:

Web site	
Username	
Password	
Notes	

NAME:

Web site	
Username	
Password	
Notes	

NAME:

Web site	
Username	
Password	
Notes	

NAME:

Web site	
Username	
Password	
Notes	

NAME:

Web site	
Username	
Password	
Notes	

NAME:

Web site	
Username	
Password	
Notes	

B Bat

NAME:

Web site	
Username	
Password	
Notes	

NAME:

Web site	
Username	
Password	
Notes	

NAME:

Web site	
Username	
Password	
Notes	

NAME:

Web site	
Username	
Password	
Notes	

NAME:

Web site	
Username	
Password	
Notes	

NAME:

Web site	
Username	
Password	
Notes	

NAME:

Web site	
Username	
Password	
Notes	

NAME:

Web site	
Username	
Password	
Notes	

NAME:

Web site	
Username	
Password	
Notes	

NAME:

Web site	
Username	
Password	
Notes	

NAME:

Web site	
Username	
Password	
Notes	

NAME:

Web site	
Username	
Password	
Notes	

NAME:

Web site	
Username	
Password	
Notes	

NAME:

Web site	
Username	
Password	
Notes	

NAME:

Web site	
Username	
Password	
Notes	

NAME:

Web site	
Username	
Password	
Notes	

NAME:

Web site	
Username	
Password	
Notes	

NAME:

Web site	
Username	
Password	
Notes	

NAME:

Web site	
Username	
Password	
Notes	

NAME:

Web site	
Username	
Password	
Notes	

NAME:

Web site	
Username	
Password	
Notes	

C Cat

NAME:	
Web site	
Username	
Password	
Notes	

NAME:	
Web site	
Username	
Password	
Notes	

NAME:	
Web site	
Username	
Password	
Notes	

NAME:

Web site	
Username	
Password	
Notes	

NAME:

Web site	
Username	
Password	
Notes	

NAME:

Web site	
Username	
Password	
Notes	

NAME:

Web site	
Username	
Password	
Notes	

NAME:

Web site	
Username	
Password	
Notes	

NAME:

Web site	
Username	
Password	
Notes	

NAME:

Web site	
Username	
Password	
Notes	

NAME:

Web site	
Username	
Password	
Notes	

NAME:

Web site	
Username	
Password	
Notes	

NAME:

Web site	
Username	
Password	
Notes	

NAME:

Web site	
Username	
Password	
Notes	

NAME:

Web site	
Username	
Password	
Notes	

NAME:

Web site	
Username	
Password	
Notes	

NAME:

Web site	
Username	
Password	
Notes	

NAME:

Web site	
Username	
Password	
Notes	

NAME:

Web site	
Username	
Password	
Notes	

NAME:

Web site	
Username	
Password	
Notes	

NAME:

Web site	
Username	
Password	
Notes	

D Dog

NAME:

Web site	
Username	
Password	
Notes	

NAME:

Web site	
Username	
Password	
Notes	

NAME:

Web site	
Username	
Password	
Notes	

NAME:

Web site	
Username	
Password	
Notes	

NAME:

Web site	
Username	
Password	
Notes	

NAME:

Web site	
Username	
Password	
Notes	

NAME:

Web site	
Username	
Password	
Notes	

NAME:

Web site	
Username	
Password	
Notes	

NAME:

Web site	
Username	
Password	
Notes	

NAME:

Web site	
Username	
Password	
Notes	

NAME:

Web site	
Username	
Password	
Notes	

NAME:

Web site	
Username	
Password	
Notes	

NAME:

Web site	
Username	
Password	
Notes	

NAME:

Web site	
Username	
Password	
Notes	

NAME:

Web site	
Username	
Password	
Notes	

NAME:

Web site	
Username	
Password	
Notes	

NAME:

Web site	
Username	
Password	
Notes	

NAME:

Web site	
Username	
Password	
Notes	

NAME:

Web site	
Username	
Password	
Notes	

NAME:

Web site	
Username	
Password	
Notes	

NAME:

Web site	
Username	
Password	
Notes	

E Egg

NAME:	
Web site	
Username	
Password	
Notes	

NAME:	
Web site	
Username	
Password	
Notes	

NAME:	
Web site	
Username	
Password	
Notes	

NAME:

Web site	
Username	
Password	
Notes	

NAME:

Web site	
Username	
Password	
Notes	

NAME:

Web site	
Username	
Password	
Notes	

NAME:

Web site	
Username	
Password	
Notes	

NAME:

Web site	
Username	
Password	
Notes	

NAME:

Web site	
Username	
Password	
Notes	

NAME:	
Web site	
Username	
Password	
Notes	

NAME:	
Web site	
Username	
Password	
Notes	

NAME:	
Web site	
Username	
Password	
Notes	

NAME:

Web site	
Username	
Password	
Notes	

NAME:

Web site	
Username	
Password	
Notes	

NAME:

Web site	
Username	
Password	
Notes	

NAME:

Web site	
Username	
Password	
Notes	

NAME:

Web site	
Username	
Password	
Notes	

NAME:

Web site	
Username	
Password	
Notes	

NAME:	
Web site	
Username	
Password	
Notes	

NAME:	
Web site	
Username	
Password	
Notes	

NAME:	
Web site	
Username	
Password	
Notes	

F Fox

NAME:	
Web site	
Username	
Password	
Notes	

NAME:	
Web site	
Username	
Password	
Notes	

NAME:	
Web site	
Username	
Password	
Notes	

NAME:

Web site	
Username	
Password	
Notes	

NAME:

Web site	
Username	
Password	
Notes	

NAME:

Web site	
Username	
Password	
Notes	

NAME:

Web site	
Username	
Password	
Notes	

NAME:

Web site	
Username	
Password	
Notes	

NAME:

Web site	
Username	
Password	
Notes	

NAME:

Web site	
Username	
Password	
Notes	

NAME:

Web site	
Username	
Password	
Notes	

NAME:

Web site	
Username	
Password	
Notes	

NAME:

Web site	
Username	
Password	
Notes	

NAME:

Web site	
Username	
Password	
Notes	

NAME:

Web site	
Username	
Password	
Notes	

NAME:	
Web site	
Username	
Password	
Notes	

NAME:	
Web site	
Username	
Password	
Notes	

NAME:	
Web site	
Username	
Password	
Notes	

NAME:

Web site	
Username	
Password	
Notes	

NAME:

Web site	
Username	
Password	
Notes	

NAME:

Web site	
Username	
Password	
Notes	

G Goose

NAME:	
Web site	
Username	
Password	
Notes	

NAME:	
Web site	
Username	
Password	
Notes	

NAME:	
Web site	
Username	
Password	
Notes	

NAME:

Web site	
Username	
Password	
Notes	

NAME:

Web site	
Username	
Password	
Notes	

NAME:

Web site	
Username	
Password	
Notes	

NAME:

Web site	
Username	
Password	
Notes	

NAME:

Web site	
Username	
Password	
Notes	

NAME:

Web site	
Username	
Password	
Notes	

NAME:

Web site	
Username	
Password	
Notes	

NAME:

Web site	
Username	
Password	
Notes	

NAME:

Web site	
Username	
Password	
Notes	

NAME:

Web site	
Username	
Password	
Notes	

NAME:

Web site	
Username	
Password	
Notes	

NAME:

Web site	
Username	
Password	
Notes	

NAME:

Web site	
Username	
Password	
Notes	

NAME:

Web site	
Username	
Password	
Notes	

NAME:

Web site	
Username	
Password	
Notes	

NAME:	
Web site	
Username	
Password	
Notes	

NAME:	
Web site	
Username	
Password	
Notes	

NAME:	
Web site	
Username	
Password	
Notes	

H House

NAME:	
Web site	
Username	
Password	
Notes	

NAME:	
Web site	
Username	
Password	
Notes	

NAME:	
Web site	
Username	
Password	
Notes	

NAME:

Web site	
Username	
Password	
Notes	

NAME:

Web site	
Username	
Password	
Notes	

NAME:

Web site	
Username	
Password	
Notes	

NAME:

Web site	
Username	
Password	
Notes	

NAME:

Web site	
Username	
Password	
Notes	

NAME:

Web site	
Username	
Password	
Notes	

NAME:	
Web site	
Username	
Password	
Notes	

NAME:	
Web site	
Username	
Password	
Notes	

NAME:	
Web site	
Username	
Password	
Notes	

NAME:

Web site	
Username	
Password	
Notes	

NAME:

Web site	
Username	
Password	
Notes	

NAME:

Web site	
Username	
Password	
Notes	

NAME:	
Web site	
Username	
Password	
Notes	

NAME:	
Web site	
Username	
Password	
Notes	

NAME:	
Web site	
Username	
Password	
Notes	

NAME:

Web site	
Username	
Password	
Notes	

NAME:

Web site	
Username	
Password	
Notes	

NAME:

Web site	
Username	
Password	
Notes	

I Ice

NAME:	
Web site	
Username	
Password	
Notes	

NAME:	
Web site	
Username	
Password	
Notes	

NAME:	
Web site	
Username	
Password	
Notes	

NAME:

Web site	
Username	
Password	
Notes	

NAME:

Web site	
Username	
Password	
Notes	

NAME:

Web site	
Username	
Password	
Notes	

NAME:

Web site	
Username	
Password	
Notes	

NAME:

Web site	
Username	
Password	
Notes	

NAME:

Web site	
Username	
Password	
Notes	

NAME:

Web site	
Username	
Password	
Notes	

NAME:

Web site	
Username	
Password	
Notes	

NAME:

Web site	
Username	
Password	
Notes	

NAME:

Web site	
Username	
Password	
Notes	

NAME:

Web site	
Username	
Password	
Notes	

NAME:

Web site	
Username	
Password	
Notes	

NAME:

Web site	
Username	
Password	
Notes	

NAME:

Web site	
Username	
Password	
Notes	

NAME:

Web site	
Username	
Password	
Notes	

NAME:

Web site	
Username	
Password	
Notes	

NAME:

Web site	
Username	
Password	
Notes	

NAME:

Web site	
Username	
Password	
Notes	

J Jazz

NAME:

Web site	
Username	
Password	
Notes	

NAME:

Web site	
Username	
Password	
Notes	

NAME:

Web site	
Username	
Password	
Notes	

NAME:

Web site	
Username	
Password	
Notes	

NAME:

Web site	
Username	
Password	
Notes	

NAME:

Web site	
Username	
Password	
Notes	

NAME:

Web site	
Username	
Password	
Notes	

NAME:

Web site	
Username	
Password	
Notes	

NAME:

Web site	
Username	
Password	
Notes	

NAME:

Web site	
Username	
Password	
Notes	

NAME:

Web site	
Username	
Password	
Notes	

NAME:

Web site	
Username	
Password	
Notes	

NAME:

Web site	
Username	
Password	
Notes	

NAME:

Web site	
Username	
Password	
Notes	

NAME:

Web site	
Username	
Password	
Notes	

NAME:

Web site	
Username	
Password	
Notes	

NAME:

Web site	
Username	
Password	
Notes	

NAME:

Web site	
Username	
Password	
Notes	

NAME:

Web site	
Username	
Password	
Notes	

NAME:

Web site	
Username	
Password	
Notes	

NAME:

Web site	
Username	
Password	
Notes	

K King

NAME:	
Web site	
Username	
Password	
Notes	

NAME:	
Web site	
Username	
Password	
Notes	

NAME:	
Web site	
Username	
Password	
Notes	

NAME:

Web site	
Username	
Password	
Notes	

NAME:

Web site	
Username	
Password	
Notes	

NAME:

Web site	
Username	
Password	
Notes	

NAME:	
Web site	
Username	
Password	
Notes	

NAME:	
Web site	
Username	
Password	
Notes	

NAME:	
Web site	
Username	
Password	
Notes	

NAME:

Web site	
Username	
Password	
Notes	

NAME:

Web site	
Username	
Password	
Notes	

NAME:

Web site	
Username	
Password	
Notes	

NAME:

Web site	
Username	
Password	
Notes	

NAME:

Web site	
Username	
Password	
Notes	

NAME:

Web site	
Username	
Password	
Notes	

NAME:

Web site	
Username	
Password	
Notes	

NAME:

Web site	
Username	
Password	
Notes	

NAME:

Web site	
Username	
Password	
Notes	

NAME:

Web site	
Username	
Password	
Notes	

NAME:

Web site	
Username	
Password	
Notes	

NAME:

Web site	
Username	
Password	
Notes	

L Lock

NAME:

Web site	
Username	
Password	
Notes	

NAME:

Web site	
Username	
Password	
Notes	

NAME:

Web site	
Username	
Password	
Notes	

NAME:	
Web site	
Username	
Password	
Notes	

NAME:	
Web site	
Username	
Password	
Notes	

NAME:	
Web site	
Username	
Password	
Notes	

NAME:

Web site	
Username	
Password	
Notes	

NAME:

Web site	
Username	
Password	
Notes	

NAME:

Web site	
Username	
Password	
Notes	

NAME:

Web site	
Username	
Password	
Notes	

NAME:

Web site	
Username	
Password	
Notes	

NAME:

Web site	
Username	
Password	
Notes	

NAME:

Web site	
Username	
Password	
Notes	

NAME:

Web site	
Username	
Password	
Notes	

NAME:

Web site	
Username	
Password	
Notes	

NAME:

Web site	
Username	
Password	
Notes	

NAME:

Web site	
Username	
Password	
Notes	

NAME:

Web site	
Username	
Password	
Notes	

NAME:

Web site	
Username	
Password	
Notes	

NAME:

Web site	
Username	
Password	
Notes	

NAME:

Web site	
Username	
Password	
Notes	

M Moose

NAME:

Web site	
Username	
Password	
Notes	

NAME:

Web site	
Username	
Password	
Notes	

NAME:

Web site	
Username	
Password	
Notes	

NAME:

Web site	
Username	
Password	
Notes	

NAME:

Web site	
Username	
Password	
Notes	

NAME:

Web site	
Username	
Password	
Notes	

NAME:

Web site	
Username	
Password	
Notes	

NAME:

Web site	
Username	
Password	
Notes	

NAME:

Web site	
Username	
Password	
Notes	

NAME:

Web site	
Username	
Password	
Notes	

NAME:

Web site	
Username	
Password	
Notes	

NAME:

Web site	
Username	
Password	
Notes	

NAME:

Web site	
Username	
Password	
Notes	

NAME:

Web site	
Username	
Password	
Notes	

NAME:

Web site	
Username	
Password	
Notes	

NAME:

Web site	
Username	
Password	
Notes	

NAME:

Web site	
Username	
Password	
Notes	

NAME:

Web site	
Username	
Password	
Notes	

NAME:

Web site	
Username	
Password	
Notes	

NAME:

Web site	
Username	
Password	
Notes	

NAME:

Web site	
Username	
Password	
Notes	

N Nest

NAME:	
Web site	
Username	
Password	
Notes	

NAME:	
Web site	
Username	
Password	
Notes	

NAME:	
Web site	
Username	
Password	
Notes	

NAME:

Web site	
Username	
Password	
Notes	

NAME:

Web site	
Username	
Password	
Notes	

NAME:

Web site	
Username	
Password	
Notes	

NAME:

Web site	
Username	
Password	
Notes	

NAME:

Web site	
Username	
Password	
Notes	

NAME:

Web site	
Username	
Password	
Notes	

NAME:

Web site	
Username	
Password	
Notes	

NAME:

Web site	
Username	
Password	
Notes	

NAME:

Web site	
Username	
Password	
Notes	

NAME:	
Web site	
Username	
Password	
Notes	

NAME:	
Web site	
Username	
Password	
Notes	

NAME:	
Web site	
Username	
Password	
Notes	

NAME:

Web site	
Username	
Password	
Notes	

NAME:

Web site	
Username	
Password	
Notes	

NAME:

Web site	
Username	
Password	
Notes	

NAME:

Web site	
Username	
Password	
Notes	

NAME:

Web site	
Username	
Password	
Notes	

NAME:

Web site	
Username	
Password	
Notes	

O Orange

NAME:	
Web site	
Username	
Password	
Notes	

NAME:	
Web site	
Username	
Password	
Notes	

NAME:	
Web site	
Username	
Password	
Notes	

NAME:

Web site	
Username	
Password	
Notes	

NAME:

Web site	
Username	
Password	
Notes	

NAME:

Web site	
Username	
Password	
Notes	

NAME:

Web site	
Username	
Password	
Notes	

NAME:

Web site	
Username	
Password	
Notes	

NAME:

Web site	
Username	
Password	
Notes	

NAME:

Web site	
Username	
Password	
Notes	

NAME:

Web site	
Username	
Password	
Notes	

NAME:

Web site	
Username	
Password	
Notes	

NAME:

Web site	
Username	
Password	
Notes	

NAME:

Web site	
Username	
Password	
Notes	

NAME:

Web site	
Username	
Password	
Notes	

NAME:

Web site	
Username	
Password	
Notes	

NAME:

Web site	
Username	
Password	
Notes	

NAME:

Web site	
Username	
Password	
Notes	

NAME:	
Web site	
Username	
Password	
Notes	

NAME:	
Web site	
Username	
Password	
Notes	

NAME:	
Web site	
Username	
Password	
Notes	

P Papaya

NAME:	
Web site	
Username	
Password	
Notes	

NAME:	
Web site	
Username	
Password	
Notes	

NAME:	
Web site	
Username	
Password	
Notes	

NAME:

Web site	
Username	
Password	
Notes	

NAME:

Web site	
Username	
Password	
Notes	

NAME:

Web site	
Username	
Password	
Notes	

NAME:

Web site	
Username	
Password	
Notes	

NAME:

Web site	
Username	
Password	
Notes	

NAME:

Web site	
Username	
Password	
Notes	

NAME:	
Web site	
Username	
Password	
Notes	

NAME:	
Web site	
Username	
Password	
Notes	

NAME:	
Web site	
Username	
Password	
Notes	

NAME:

Web site	
Username	
Password	
Notes	

NAME:

Web site	
Username	
Password	
Notes	

NAME:

Web site	
Username	
Password	
Notes	

NAME:

Web site	
Username	
Password	
Notes	

NAME:

Web site	
Username	
Password	
Notes	

NAME:

Web site	
Username	
Password	
Notes	

NAME:

Web site	
Username	
Password	
Notes	

NAME:

Web site	
Username	
Password	
Notes	

NAME:

Web site	
Username	
Password	
Notes	

Q Queen

NAME:	
Web site	
Username	
Password	
Notes	

NAME:	
Web site	
Username	
Password	
Notes	

NAME:	
Web site	
Username	
Password	
Notes	

NAME:

Web site	
Username	
Password	
Notes	

NAME:

Web site	
Username	
Password	
Notes	

NAME:

Web site	
Username	
Password	
Notes	

NAME:

Web site	
Username	
Password	
Notes	

NAME:

Web site	
Username	
Password	
Notes	

NAME:

Web site	
Username	
Password	
Notes	

NAME:

Web site	
Username	
Password	
Notes	

NAME:

Web site	
Username	
Password	
Notes	

NAME:

Web site	
Username	
Password	
Notes	

NAME:

Web site	
Username	
Password	
Notes	

NAME:

Web site	
Username	
Password	
Notes	

NAME:

Web site	
Username	
Password	
Notes	

NAME:

Web site	
Username	
Password	
Notes	

NAME:

Web site	
Username	
Password	
Notes	

NAME:

Web site	
Username	
Password	
Notes	

NAME:

Web site	
Username	
Password	
Notes	

NAME:

Web site	
Username	
Password	
Notes	

NAME:

Web site	
Username	
Password	
Notes	

R Rooster

NAME:	
Web site	
Username	
Password	
Notes	

NAME:	
Web site	
Username	
Password	
Notes	

NAME:	
Web site	
Username	
Password	
Notes	

NAME:

Web site	
Username	
Password	
Notes	

NAME:

Web site	
Username	
Password	
Notes	

NAME:

Web site	
Username	
Password	
Notes	

NAME:

Web site	
Username	
Password	
Notes	

NAME:

Web site	
Username	
Password	
Notes	

NAME:

Web site	
Username	
Password	
Notes	

NAME:

Web site	
Username	
Password	
Notes	

NAME:

Web site	
Username	
Password	
Notes	

NAME:

Web site	
Username	
Password	
Notes	

NAME:

Web site	
Username	
Password	
Notes	

NAME:

Web site	
Username	
Password	
Notes	

NAME:

Web site	
Username	
Password	
Notes	

NAME:	
Web site	
Username	
Password	
Notes	

NAME:	
Web site	
Username	
Password	
Notes	

NAME:	
Web site	
Username	
Password	
Notes	

NAME:

Web site	
Username	
Password	
Notes	

NAME:

Web site	
Username	
Password	
Notes	

NAME:

Web site	
Username	
Password	
Notes	

S Snake

NAME:	
Web site	
Username	
Password	
Notes	

NAME:	
Web site	
Username	
Password	
Notes	

NAME:	
Web site	
Username	
Password	
Notes	

NAME:

Web site	
Username	
Password	
Notes	

NAME:

Web site	
Username	
Password	
Notes	

NAME:

Web site	
Username	
Password	
Notes	

NAME:

Web site	
Username	
Password	
Notes	

NAME:

Web site	
Username	
Password	
Notes	

NAME:

Web site	
Username	
Password	
Notes	

NAME:

Web site	
Username	
Password	
Notes	

NAME:

Web site	
Username	
Password	
Notes	

NAME:

Web site	
Username	
Password	
Notes	

NAME:

Web site	
Username	
Password	
Notes	

NAME:

Web site	
Username	
Password	
Notes	

NAME:

Web site	
Username	
Password	
Notes	

NAME:

Web site	
Username	
Password	
Notes	

NAME:

Web site	
Username	
Password	
Notes	

NAME:

Web site	
Username	
Password	
Notes	

NAME:

Web site	
Username	
Password	
Notes	

NAME:

Web site	
Username	
Password	
Notes	

NAME:

Web site	
Username	
Password	
Notes	

T Turtle

NAME:

Web site	
Username	
Password	
Notes	

NAME:

Web site	
Username	
Password	
Notes	

NAME:

Web site	
Username	
Password	
Notes	

NAME:

Web site	
Username	
Password	
Notes	

NAME:

Web site	
Username	
Password	
Notes	

NAME:

Web site	
Username	
Password	
Notes	

NAME:

Web site	
Username	
Password	
Notes	

NAME:

Web site	
Username	
Password	
Notes	

NAME:

Web site	
Username	
Password	
Notes	

NAME:

Web site	
Username	
Password	
Notes	

NAME:

Web site	
Username	
Password	
Notes	

NAME:

Web site	
Username	
Password	
Notes	

NAME:

Web site	
Username	
Password	
Notes	

NAME:

Web site	
Username	
Password	
Notes	

NAME:

Web site	
Username	
Password	
Notes	

NAME:

Web site	
Username	
Password	
Notes	

NAME:

Web site	
Username	
Password	
Notes	

NAME:

Web site	
Username	
Password	
Notes	

NAME:	
Web site	
Username	
Password	
Notes	

NAME:	
Web site	
Username	
Password	
Notes	

NAME:	
Web site	
Username	
Password	
Notes	

U Union

NAME:	
Web site	
Username	
Password	
Notes	

NAME:	
Web site	
Username	
Password	
Notes	

NAME:	
Web site	
Username	
Password	
Notes	

NAME:

Web site	
Username	
Password	
Notes	

NAME:

Web site	
Username	
Password	
Notes	

NAME:

Web site	
Username	
Password	
Notes	

NAME:

Web site	
Username	
Password	
Notes	

NAME:

Web site	
Username	
Password	
Notes	

NAME:

Web site	
Username	
Password	
Notes	

NAME:

Web site	
Username	
Password	
Notes	

NAME:

Web site	
Username	
Password	
Notes	

NAME:

Web site	
Username	
Password	
Notes	

NAME:

Web site	
Username	
Password	
Notes	

NAME:

Web site	
Username	
Password	
Notes	

NAME:

Web site	
Username	
Password	
Notes	

NAME:

Web site	
Username	
Password	
Notes	

NAME:

Web site	
Username	
Password	
Notes	

NAME:

Web site	
Username	
Password	
Notes	

NAME:

Web site	
Username	
Password	
Notes	

NAME:

Web site	
Username	
Password	
Notes	

NAME:

Web site	
Username	
Password	
Notes	

V Victory

NAME:

Web site	
Username	
Password	
Notes	

NAME:

Web site	
Username	
Password	
Notes	

NAME:

Web site	
Username	
Password	
Notes	

NAME:

Web site	
Username	
Password	
Notes	

NAME:

Web site	
Username	
Password	
Notes	

NAME:

Web site	
Username	
Password	
Notes	

NAME:

Web site	
Username	
Password	
Notes	

NAME:

Web site	
Username	
Password	
Notes	

NAME:

Web site	
Username	
Password	
Notes	

NAME:

Web site	
Username	
Password	
Notes	

NAME:

Web site	
Username	
Password	
Notes	

NAME:

Web site	
Username	
Password	
Notes	

NAME:

Web site	
Username	
Password	
Notes	

NAME:

Web site	
Username	
Password	
Notes	

NAME:

Web site	
Username	
Password	
Notes	

NAME:

Web site	
Username	
Password	
Notes	

NAME:

Web site	
Username	
Password	
Notes	

NAME:

Web site	
Username	
Password	
Notes	

NAME:

Web site	
Username	
Password	
Notes	

NAME:

Web site	
Username	
Password	
Notes	

NAME:

Web site	
Username	
Password	
Notes	

W Wool

NAME:	
Web site	
Username	
Password	
Notes	

NAME:	
Web site	
Username	
Password	
Notes	

NAME:	
Web site	
Username	
Password	
Notes	

NAME:

Web site	
Username	
Password	
Notes	

NAME:

Web site	
Username	
Password	
Notes	

NAME:

Web site	
Username	
Password	
Notes	

NAME:

Web site	
Username	
Password	
Notes	

NAME:

Web site	
Username	
Password	
Notes	

NAME:

Web site	
Username	
Password	
Notes	

NAME:

Web site	
Username	
Password	
Notes	

NAME:

Web site	
Username	
Password	
Notes	

NAME:

Web site	
Username	
Password	
Notes	

NAME:

Web site	
Username	
Password	
Notes	

NAME:

Web site	
Username	
Password	
Notes	

NAME:

Web site	
Username	
Password	
Notes	

NAME:

Web site	
Username	
Password	
Notes	

NAME:

Web site	
Username	
Password	
Notes	

NAME:

Web site	
Username	
Password	
Notes	

NAME:

Web site	
Username	
Password	
Notes	

NAME:

Web site	
Username	
Password	
Notes	

NAME:

Web site	
Username	
Password	
Notes	

X X-ray

NAME:	
Web site	
Username	
Password	
Notes	

NAME:	
Web site	
Username	
Password	
Notes	

NAME:	
Web site	
Username	
Password	
Notes	

NAME:

Web site	
Username	
Password	
Notes	

NAME:

Web site	
Username	
Password	
Notes	

NAME:

Web site	
Username	
Password	
Notes	

NAME:

Web site	
Username	
Password	
Notes	

NAME:

Web site	
Username	
Password	
Notes	

NAME:

Web site	
Username	
Password	
Notes	

NAME:

Web site	
Username	
Password	
Notes	

NAME:

Web site	
Username	
Password	
Notes	

NAME:

Web site	
Username	
Password	
Notes	

NAME:

Web site	
Username	
Password	
Notes	

NAME:

Web site	
Username	
Password	
Notes	

NAME:

Web site	
Username	
Password	
Notes	

NAME:

Web site	
Username	
Password	
Notes	

NAME:

Web site	
Username	
Password	
Notes	

NAME:

Web site	
Username	
Password	
Notes	

NAME:

Web site	
Username	
Password	
Notes	

NAME:

Web site	
Username	
Password	
Notes	

NAME:

Web site	
Username	
Password	
Notes	

Y Yam

NAME:

Web site	
Username	
Password	
Notes	

NAME:

Web site	
Username	
Password	
Notes	

NAME:

Web site	
Username	
Password	
Notes	

NAME:

Web site	
Username	
Password	
Notes	

NAME:

Web site	
Username	
Password	
Notes	

NAME:

Web site	
Username	
Password	
Notes	

NAME:

Web site	
Username	
Password	
Notes	

NAME:

Web site	
Username	
Password	
Notes	

NAME:

Web site	
Username	
Password	
Notes	

NAME:

Web site	
Username	
Password	
Notes	

NAME:

Web site	
Username	
Password	
Notes	

NAME:

Web site	
Username	
Password	
Notes	

NAME:

Web site	
Username	
Password	
Notes	

NAME:

Web site	
Username	
Password	
Notes	

NAME:

Web site	
Username	
Password	
Notes	

NAME:

Web site	
Username	
Password	
Notes	

NAME:

Web site	
Username	
Password	
Notes	

NAME:

Web site	
Username	
Password	
Notes	

NAME:

Web site	
Username	
Password	
Notes	

NAME:

Web site	
Username	
Password	
Notes	

NAME:

Web site	
Username	
Password	
Notes	

Z Zoo

NAME:

Web site	
Username	
Password	
Notes	

NAME:

Web site	
Username	
Password	
Notes	

NAME:

Web site	
Username	
Password	
Notes	

NAME:

Web site	
Username	
Password	
Notes	

NAME:

Web site	
Username	
Password	
Notes	

NAME:

Web site	
Username	
Password	
Notes	

NAME:

Web site	
Username	
Password	
Notes	

NAME:

Web site	
Username	
Password	
Notes	

NAME:

Web site	
Username	
Password	
Notes	

NAME:

Web site	
Username	
Password	
Notes	

NAME:

Web site	
Username	
Password	
Notes	

NAME:

Web site	
Username	
Password	
Notes	

NAME:	
Web site	
Username	
Password	
Notes	

NAME:	
Web site	
Username	
Password	
Notes	

NAME:	
Web site	
Username	
Password	
Notes	

NAME:	
Web site	
Username	
Password	
Notes	

NAME:	
Web site	
Username	
Password	
Notes	

NAME:	
Web site	
Username	
Password	
Notes	

NAME:

Web site	
Username	
Password	
Notes	

NAME:

Web site	
Username	
Password	
Notes	

NAME:

Web site	
Username	
Password	
Notes	

WiFi Networks

WiFi is everywhere now—McDonalds, Barnes and Noble, and of course Starbucks.

Location	
WiFi name (SSID)	
password	

Location	
WiFi name (SSID)	
password	

Location	
WiFi name (SSID)	
password	

Location	
WiFi name (SSID)	
password	

Location	
WiFi name (SSID)	
password	

Location	
WiFi name (SSID)	
password	

Location	
WiFi name (SSID)	
password	

Location	
WiFi name (SSID)	
password	

License Keys/Serial

Product Name	Serial Number or License Key

Product Name	Serial Number or License Key

Product Name	Serial Number or License Key

Product Name	Serial Number or License Key

Other Accounts

These are for your other accounts that don't necessarily fit in the categories in the previous sections.

Account Name	Account Info

Account Name	Account Info

Account Name	Account Info

Account Name	Account Info

Account Name	Account Info

Account Name	Account Info

Feedback

If you have suggestions to improve this book, don't hesitate to contact me at forlanda@gmail.com.